# American Amen

# American Amen

poems by

## Gary L. McDowell

Dream Horse Press
California

Library of Congress Cataloging-in-Publication Data:

McDowell, Gary L. (1980- )
    American Amen
        p.      cm

        ISBN 978-19357160-4-4
        1. Poetry

10 9 8 7 6 5 4 3 2 1

First Edition


Cover by Frank P. Cucciarre, Blink Concept & Design, Inc.

# Table of Contents

*Aubade*                                                            9

Lake Big Arbor Vitae                                              10

Ovaries                                                           11

The Whole of It                                                   12

Notes from a Sleepwalker                                          16

*Aubade*                                                          18

A Poem about My Father Will Always Begin
     *My Father*                          19

Apology                                                           20

The Beginnings                                                    21

Tricycle                                                          25

How to Say *I Love You*                                           26

*Aubade*                                                          27

Blackbirds                                                        28

Tornado Warning                                                   32

Nectar                                                            33

Love                                                              34

A Miscarriage Scare at Bronson Methodist                          35

*Aubade*                                                          36

My Ill-lit Something                                              37

Snorkeling                                                        38

Lake Little Arbor Vitae                                           39

A Feeding                                                         40

And She's Fallen                                                  43

All Stones Are Broken Stones                                      44

*Aubade*                                                          45

Heritage                                                          46

If you've never seen the devil                    47

Divorce                                           49

Father, there are poets                           50

Orgasm                                            52

*Aubade*                                          54

Yellow Jackets                                    55

Opera                                             56

Ninth Morning in a Row with Binoculars            57

The Nightmare Where I Walk in the Forest          59

Forever Falling Off or Out                        60

*Aubade*                                          62

DeKalb, Illinois, August 21, 2002                 63

Weather, Weather                                  64

Earth's Otherwise Silence                         65

Back Home                                         66

Painting Houses                                   67

Winter                                            69

Too Damn Perfect                                  71

Acknowledgments                                   75

*And ghosts must do again*
*What gives them pain.*

—W.H. Auden

*The boys kept reeling in.*
*Casting and reeling in. You'll never catch a fish*
*that way, you said. One caught a fish that way.*

— Robert Hass

# Aubade

*Look for me in the fat black of the Ohio night.*
*If steel, if wheat, if river, if corn,*

                               *come lay me down.*

*Back against the whirl of dark,*
*the scarf-sleeved, deep-breath dark,*

                               *look for me.*

*I walk across a patio, my dusk-purple feathers,*
*tired head—it bobs—and my bones, marrowless.*

*A body can't just die.*

                    *Night must evolve.*
*Fingers turn to wings, and though I sleep,*

                               *come lay me down.*

# Lake Big Arbor Vitae

My father either floats or sinks. I forget which, though I'm sure I know. Late April. Milky Bay.

Fishing for walleye. Eagles nest in the pines. Something builds a dam.

I put my hand in the styrofoam bait container and wait. I will fish with my own blood.

My father pisses into the bay. I hook my leech through its tail. Pull its mouth from my finger. I cast and my line fizzes.

I blow smoke rings with the cold air. My lips taste like steaming ice.

An otter barks from the shore.

Our lines bob in the bay. *This is patience.* The eagles start hunting. My father says, *watch.*

With talons stretched, the first eagle plunges his feet through the water's surface. There's barely a ripple.

# Ovaries

The body of water that cries
in search, unable to breathe.

Broken, can you ask for more?
Water crying, water

for the mouth.  It's why
we have throats.  If I am

without the body my voice
will die and shake off stars

or fall one half of a year.
I am what I fear to be. I am a loop.

# The Whole of It

I could tell you.

           How the blue-winged teal scuttles
over the grass
        and regains the water.

How the pond outside my window,
                gated and fenced—
                no kids will drown there—
     in prairie-pothole-country,
not a marsh, wetland, or flooded ditch

on a golf course.

But a shallow pond.  And when frightened, the teal
                    springs into flight.

What am I
      tethered?  What am I divorced?

———————————

So much to wish.

A poem about my grandmother,

        about watching a teal
fly to the middle of the pond, her mottled gray-brown

                body plumage,
her pale head,
      blue upper wings,

no white crescent on her face,

no white on her underwing.


A poem about nature's most efficient machines.

A poem
about missing you.

How I am lost in the-city-of-best-words,

the imagination's particulars.

The idea-man,
the-man-the-boy-who-jars-his-city

only to open it later when it rains.

I own thousands of envelopes.

I should have written you more letters.

What is solid? *What* is rather dull.

I will mail you
a poem about
the teal and her diet.

———————————

The blue-wings are the first ducks south in the fall
and the last north in the spring:

they have it right: go to the middle of a pond

                                        and sleep by night
under the moon, bills tucked and nestled into feathers.
                                        And that moon,
its trumpet-horn, subscribes to the engine: the *what* that keeps us
        from flying.

                        Do you remember

hearing that cricket-like call in the early mornings?  Out the window
                                        over your pond
not unlike my pond.  How the drake would wait patiently,

                his brown speckled breast, blackish crown,

and your coffee thinned with cream,
the sun off the water, your hummingbird feeder swinging

                                        in the garden.

——————————————

Time, it seems to me,

is more the-halls-of-all-the-pretty-things that fly,
        leaves us earliest in the morning

                        without a window to call our own,

                        and I am the-boy-who-lost-

himself watching that blue-winged teal
          circle the pond,

and all that's left in her wake is the water.

# Notes from a Sleepwalker

My jowls astound you. I am alive. Amen. It is my habit.

I know that a woman who has no legs cannot *walk all over me*. Knees are confounding, not round, neither are they square. What I know impresses me. I am seabird. Land bird. I am time. I sometimes pretend to be mad. I do this because I think too much.

The toreador always weeps before killing the bull. Amen.

I am the urge of my unconscious mind.

Every penis has a man. What I don't know is just as complicated. The earth is cooling down. It is still warm, but not for long. Though I dislike geography as I dislike frontiers.

For me, the earth is one single state. It is the head. And I am alive as long as there is fire in that head. Amen.

My hands move simply, but the movements of a monkey's hands are immense. A monkey is stupid. I am stupid too, but I have sense. I like to speak in tongues because I am a tongue myself. It pleases me to no end.

Just listen to these waves. Amen.

I am spiritual food. In water there are rainbows. Light. A bird without wings is an airplane without feathers. This is not a metaphor for fear.

Sometimes I make myself nervous on purpose. One time, I allowed a man to make love to me. He stretched me and enjoyed me. He loved little boys but did not love me. No one came to my rescue.

Woman. Despite ribs. If I am wrong, I will learn what my body is for. I am angular, musical. I am a comet. Amen.

I like to be talked about. My mother nourished me with her own milk. Amen. I feel my secret. It's raw like beef. Like a séance. I understood everything as a child and now cannot count, cannot sleep.

Sleight-of-hand, an extreme close-up of coal. Miners and their pails are syllabically boring. I am a zoom shot of a nude portrait, the cross-section—Amen—of a honeycomb.

I am the Museum of Articulation, dinosaur bones and all. I am the first time I got an erection on purpose. Some things are better when your mind is clear.

I am unashamed of how I taste. Livers are enduring. I drink often to that. I drink often to the fact that I was conceived. What is new is unkempt. Amen. I am a veiled neck. I am clasped. I am every circle between our hands.

## Aubade

And it's morning, flash-in-the-what's-left-of-night:

                                        spun-out stars
and blind crickets, legs still beating.

Hidden in the ragweed of late summer
is remedy and the teeth of dead raccoons,

            ten cents for a soda can,

and deer feeding or mating in the backyard.

We are in reverie, the orbits of the planets:
time-symmetrical.

I was once told that deer antlers,
                                even after death,
are warm to the touch.

## A Poem about My Father Will Always Begin *My Father*

My father never told me
I limped a long time
after my bones had knit,
favored one leg more
than the other, egged myself
forward, one knee knotted,
never told me my fists
were too small for fighting,
too small to be blamed
for violence: the grasp and tug
at my mother's hair,
that tug to pull myself closer,
to grasp something other than air.
My father never told me
I was a body, I was a herder,
never told me that when bitten
I should swear, swear.
A poem about my father
will always begin *in October*.
In October, we flew kites
in the frantic rush of winds.
My hawk never had its feathers,
his eagle never lost
its feathers. Our birds
soared but never threaded
our story to another story,
never forgot who we were,
us, me and my father,
when I was young.

# Apology

*Sorry, Sorry, Sorry.*
My father said that word so many times,
I thought it meant Mother.

# The Beginnings

The boys pretend to know
why the illusionist pulls silks from his sleeves.

How he does his tricks is a story
        the boys know the ending to:
                                vanishing is less
magical than reappearing, more necessary than sewing
extra pockets in suit coats.

What I want
is to tear a heaven for those little boys
                                and the monsters
they'll become,

tear a heaven from some book.

As I watch them, I am free of my shy needs.

————————————

At the fair the conjuror's son
        (plain and pale)
lists and roars with the audience
                        a new history

        (but for him the same),

one predetermined yet gentle,
one desired like canvas:

                        prude but worth mentioning.

How unending it must be, the son
of a conjuror.

How *away* could never be *near*,
how his slim frame couldn't vanish.

Running would lose its purpose.
        Hiding: no longer a game.

*The secrets he must keep.*

———————————

Two days the flower I bought myself at the fair
        lives without water.

                I cried for that conjuror's child.

Where does a boy bury what hurts him?
                When does a man
know he's grown too far?

From home?
From beginnings?

        Home demands the comforts of night,
the banalities of morning.

Leaving is morning turning to night,

                        the day missing

in-between, the day

                              of curtained mornings
when fathers and their lovers
                    (when sons hidden in closets)
match their breathing
                              with train-whistles.


———————————————


          And in the summer, before the rains
or during the rains,

how we galloped
                    through the woods,
our feet wet and growing,

never bored, us madmen,
never merely sons, us heavenly monsters,

          terrified
of what drifted beyond us, considered ourselves lucky,

                              ready to elude
what would happen next.


———————————————


          Not to say tradition, not to say triumph,
but to mark an inch in youth as our own:

there's something baffling about adulthood,
                    the mystery about people when they leave us,
when they rock loose,

                                        when there is no longer
any sequence.

I feel the earth under me,
          its slow rush of mud and grass,
I believe again in running after hares,
          in illusion and breakfast

                         in the middle of the day,

and I have to bang
against some concrete floor
to call myself back.

# Tricycle

The boy next door used to flip his tricycle upside down and turn the pedals with his hands. He would hold his sister's doll over the spinning tire. Her hair frayed until it curled black and burnt. One time the hair got caught in the spokes. Its head wedged between the metal fork and the hub. The doll spun in circles. The friction from the tire smudged her face and her dress ripped to bare her flat plastic chest. In the backyard I'd run my hands over his sister's chest and try to stop her flesh from burning under the spinning wheel.

# How to Say *I Love You*
### *after Keats*


On evenings when my dogs and I circle the block,
if I am guilty of anything,

it's of being distracted by the streetlamp.

      I am visible in it.

If I look directly at the lamp, I can't see the stars.
I don't need the stars anymore?
                    I used to think

*I'd cavern you, and grotto you, waterfall you,*
*and immense-rock you,*         *solitude you*

until rain gristled the evening, lit
our roof to singing—

And of thinking too hard about what to say
      when I walk through the door:

my wife: *welcome home high-wires*
*and habitual nightmares, lonely woes*
               *and wooden shoes!*

# Aubade

*Sunlight through clouds isn't light but a stroke*
*of dark.*
        *A picnic of strawberries and bread*

*and rain: how much like love is that?  Hip-high*
*grass, yellow flowers that smell of wind and work,*

           *notches in roadside fence-posts:*
*children waiting for the school bus.*

*Thunder has never torn a bird from a telephone pole,*
*but darkness, the crow's own shade of purple—*

*you wake before sunrise to feed the winter-robins*
*left-over bread.*

# Blackbirds

I've never seen him without a beard,
                              but the sputtering light of the fire
helps me imagine
how he looks clean-shaven.

        Pine logs settle and burn, snapping,
                              at the bottom of the fire pit.
Heat on my forehead; the hair on my knuckles

stands up, pulled straight by heat.

The breeze swirls around the fire, throwing bright ash
in our laps.

Above us, night has spread;
                        the star's vibrance
this far from the city.

        My father holds a rifle in his lap, polished
and unused for over ten years; we are quiet.

Where have we been and how is it we've never lost our way?

_____

Another log burns in the fire,
                        and still I wish I could've grown a beard,
or even a passable shadow

        to hide my sweat

as we cleared grandfather's house of his belongings,
kept only what he loved:

a circular saw, pictures of my grandmother,
a few crappies mounted on plaques, and his rifle.

      My father didn't sweat at all,

                  didn't speak on the drive home,
only nodded his head to the radio.

The fire is dimming now, and my father points
the rifle to the sky, spies through the sights,
         *that there is Ursa Minor*
*and over there*, he swings to the left and points
              South and low over the horizon,
*is Scorpius.*

———————

My grandfather: *stay away from the purple crows.*
            Their iridescent wings, black beaks
and feet like cowhide only blacker, and how they'd mimic
    the cocking of our rifles, our laughs,

and the nightly applause for Johnny Carson.

My father: *crows—too quick to shoo away, too illegal to shoot.*

It was at our cabin in Arbor Vitae, Wisconsin
where my father and grandfather would sit for hours
            watching blackbirds,

where I'd put my father's rifle to my shoulder,
lean my head against the butt stock,

and my father, the graceful way he'd pull

the rifle from my hands

and tell me, *blackbirds, son.  Shoot only the blackbirds.*

————————————

My grandfather a boy, the rifle strapped to his shoulder,
the leather rough and hot.
A brown satchel on his other shoulder,

and later, fifteen years later,

he'd show my father how to hold

a rifle steady against his cheek,
show him the right way to stoke a fire on the lake shore,

show him, when at the cabin, how to call home every third day,
to check-in with Grandma.

My father a boy, following his father into the woods.
The undergrowth along the backyard fence is burnt
just enough so they can hurdle it

and walk easily into the forest,

tracking with their cocker a flush of pheasants.

And when they're distracted

by a brace of blackbirds,
does my grandfather know to hand his son the rifle

because it will be an easy first shot

or because he remembers the smell
of gunpowder and pond water, hot leather against his skin?

Years later I'd read of the red-winged blackbirds,
                                        their scarlet shoulder patches,
their pinkish chin
and throat.

Their call from the stumps of dead oaks:
                                        an inhaled whistle,
a breath not quite fulfilled
like a man casting and casting his bait into the lake—

# Tornado Warning

All the dirt and dust I've wiped from the TV over the years,
the cans of Lysol emptied in the bathrooms

(our bedroom on certain nights),
and all I can think of is how many times I've left this body
for some other body that, despite my best wishes, had irreversible constraints.

I spent hours of my childhood standing in doorways
waiting to hear a freight train lift my house

from the ground,
rattle the windows rubbery and insubstantial.

I couldn't stop myself from pressing
the backs of my hands hard against the door frame,

pinning my wrists, enjoying the resistance,
and when the sirens stopped, when the air smelled

like dry dirt again,
I'd step away and relax my arms, feel them

rise from my sides to parallel
the floor, drifting upward as though filled with sky.

# Nectar

I found my history in the tiny
bones of a hummingbird, beating heart
that couldn't fill a thimble with its blood.
Subtle feet and soft beak,
never again to fly sideways
or beat wings faster
than a prayer can leave.

Hummingbird, fly into my mouth and lay
your head under my tongue.
Let me turn your death
against my teeth
and weigh it—
weigh myself.

# Love

The taste of bitten shoulders,

                               if shoulders could be bitten.

You're aged honey,

                 a shaken snowglobe.

        Thirst is cesarean: I'd love to draw your hips,

if hips could be drawn.

I don't know how to draw.

*How* takes patience.  I am tethered.

You'll leave me for the mystery

                       of smoke, but I will button

          my tongue to yours, and say, *there is danger in remembering*:

I want to shave your head.

Thieve you, tumble you,

wrap you in my heat and slip.

# A Miscarriage Scare At Bronson Methodist

*after John Rybicki*

Lord, we won't cry,
We'll carry our numb body

Home to our warm bed,
Rest our head, rest

Our head and be lamed
By our thoughts of death.

Lord, take what you've come for
And leave her to her body's noise:

No beasts would live there anymore.
No other beasts anymore.

# Aubade

Forty-four hours of rain
                    and the frogs have moved into our garage.
People are floating down the Mississippi: the swells,
the great weight of mud.  They slop off

in Illinois, maybe Missouri, confused, broken over rocks.

The willows
            sing low to the ground,
sway heavy in the heavy winds.

———————————

Roethke asked, do maimed gods walk?
I say they do,
            and the rain would like to prove it.

———————————

From my child's room: the cramp of colic, a crying
                                    like weather saws,
reversed—and it will not be his last flood.

I will shed my clothes
            to slow my daemon down,

stand open-mouthed in the rain
                    and coax my voice to hardening.

# My Ill-lit Something

All the voices that unchain our fingers from the hurt—

something tells me faith will play a part,
                              the part of grammarian, negligent father-figure,
or I'll scare easily and forget the canoe, the rockened bottom
of the lake, and push off shore,

                              float on my belly
under the sun, intensity of light and greed,

the absence of swimming.  There's always a poem
in my lake,
          a swimmer in my ill-lit something.

# Snorkeling

The distant thunder keeps beat
with the steel drummers on shore.
We push away and *The Snorkeler* eases
into the bay. Above us, gulls glide
westward ignoring the scraps of teriyaki
left by children, the spools of fried breads
and candied plums that litter the docks.
I taste salt with every breath.
Waves break against the hull, the soft
spray whisks back into our faces.
Dad holds onto the rail as the boat dips
and pushes, flails and falls.
I want to tame the water,
reweave the breakers into something smooth,
skin of a snare drum, tight and melodic.
Dad's legs, so thin and weak,
shake every time we hollow, bottom-out
in the wake of a wave. He's dying.
But we're going deeper into the thunder until the drums
drown-out and the hairs on my arms stand.
We float toward the coral, the sharp,
ragged edges of fish bones and fossilized
lobsters, to where the gulls
can't feed, too far from shore,
so instead they keen and whine.
The ocean is too cold, the lightning
will not strike us, but the boat is turning
back. Dad's gaunt hips and swollen middle
set against the steel blue storm
remind me that we're all flesh,
all boom, and I want to push him in
hard and unashamed.

# Lake Little Arbor Vitae

Fish scales and blood onto the cold basement floor.

To gut a fish, slide the knife up the belly from its ass to its gills.

If the fish is still moving, smack it on the head with a brick. And its body will straighten.

We eat fresh walleye filets coated in dehydrated potato flakes and pan-fried in butter

or cooked slowly over an open flame, the moon tiding the smoke through the fish.

Male crickets harp their wings and females flock to join them.

The birds are purple and translucent in the night. They will not cry in death. They will simply plummet to the lake and splash.

# A Feeding

He grasps the tick close to the skin of my neckline, my father's fingernails as tweezers, his steady, trained hands used to cleaning plaque

---

The electric chair
was invented by a dentist.

I want so badly to believe that's true.

And it is

---

A hot needle, a shot of vodka for my neck, for the vessel the tick has mistaken as a deer's hide, the whiteness of skin near the hairline, white like whale bones on the ocean floor

---

It will not back out on its own.

My grandfather: *pull carefully,*
*don't leave its mouthparts.*

*Relax it with the needle.*

Unfed ticks are shaped like a flat seed,
are the size of a flat seed

---

Mouthparts

is a word

———————————

And death, what it must taste like for a tick. To live on blood, mix it with one's own. And their legs, brittle. Mouths, so strong. If not squeezed to death, they rust from the inside out. Butterflies' taste sensors are in their feet. How their legs must tingle when they land on a human: so much salt

———————————

Fingernails grow two inches
per year.

I want so badly to believe that's true.

And it is

———————————

My father's fingers like—whales have baleen instead of teeth, a moustache of long bristles that hold their prey, and after forcing water out of its mouth, the whale licks krill off with its fleshy tongue—how whales strain water, swallow, as they swim, the ocean

———————————

Homogenous

is an emotion

———————————

My father forever. There is no animal bizarre enough to take man's place. How we hover over each other when injured, how we stand up to each other when wronged. Or how one man will say *I did this, I created this, and I will not let it be ruined*

———————————

I'd never known anything well enough
to witness its dying

so I held my breath,
and my father's fingers,
as nightmares do the living

# And She's Fallen

Eight months: stumbling, earlying.
     I'm fixing the doorknob:

too many hinges unhinged, not enough
light.

       I know she's bathing:

the water running, fan on high, heat
coming under the door.

And she's fallen.

Out the window: hot-air balloons
        and dust from the neighborhood diamond:

fuel me, my shoulders, help lift her.

        The weight, a river's weight:

prey to running, scorned through the night
until her knees unlock, her thighs

unrain. The child is beating, his heart.

# All Stones Are Broken Stones

Last night I dreamt of swallows
flying from her mouth:
their slanted wings left cuts in her throat.

She looked content with their expulsion,
her flesh eager and moist.
A bustle of blue backs thrusting:
the gathering of twigs and stones,
and gravity resolved in her ribcage.

They speak of fruit.
Their tail streamers scissor the fervent thread
and drink of her ashen body—

## Aubade

*I've been thinking about thinking about God*
*in my bruises:*

                    *psalm me—the congregation*
*will say nothing—*

                    *and language will have won again.*

*I will die many times before my death.*

# Heritage

thought the world hung by cords

thought the Water Beetle drudged

thought mud when all was water

thought the Natives, my Natives

thought and the animals sent birds

thought all the land was mountains

thought another world under this

thought buzzards and crayfish

thought seven hand-breadths above

thought go about in the dark

thought struck Her with a fish, bred

thought and it has been so ever since

# If you've never seen the devil

*If you've never seen the devil, look inside yourself.*

The hawk soared above her grave,

light and buoyant:
       lust before obligation,
sky before land

---

My grandmother's buried under the shadow of a maple tree.

A hawk: a poem: a poem about a hawk: no:

       *let evening come.*
*Let it come, as it will, and don't*
*be afraid*

---

The mind's fear of emptiness,
the river's plunge south.

There is no river
here in the graveyard,

yet I often see
old men in canoes,
their boned arms
just skin and sun.

Their old minds oaring,
the lines in their palms etched
and tipped like feathers

———————————

In the dream of canoes,
their passages, the hollows.

The dead don't look scared,
floating by in their caskets.

No, I've never seen the devil,
but a Ferris wheel on fire,
my grandmother frying donuts,
her apron covered in flour

# Divorce

I slept through the whole damn thing,
twelve years old: sirens and screaming.

It's never enough just to tell the story:

you have to have seen the flames, the blackened couch
shining, mirrored like onyx.

As a boy, smoke meant leaves burning,
Dad had come to gather us for the weekend.

I've told myself: *in case of fire, any god will do.*

# Father, there are poets

Father, there are poets who could learn from you

—————————

When you heard, for the first time,
Father, Lake Michigan alive,
the rush of water
into shore-rocks,

you captured it in a bottle, didn't you?

Or saw, for the first time, a firefly ignite

or touched it just

—————————

The vein in your hand leaps

      over your knuckles

when you clench your fist

—————————

Under your skin,
the wrinkles in the crook
of your elbow.
I've been tucked away there
for years at a time

—————————

The stories you told me
of great-grandfather,

his death by falling tree

——————————————

And there's us

Acreages of bones
in positions unthinkable

——————————————

In dentistry you have a term:

deciduous teeth

——————————————

One day, your body will open,
and you'll be naked
where the mourners gather
and I'll remember
how you said,
*if I had wings,*
*I wouldn't worry about*
*how far I could fly,*
*but why the fuck would I have wings?*

# Orgasm

I cannot swallow fire.
I once thought I could and so I tried.

My tongue bled
and I was still thirsty.

I waited for a circus
to come through town

with its clowns and elephants,
but it never did,

so I watched my dog
bark the alphabet.

My father once told me

*no good man lives alone*
*and all good women give head.*

I wanted to swallow fire the way my father would,
then probe the whites of his eyes with his finger,

push his eyeball until it sank back into his skull.
He kept doing this because

he knew I couldn't do it,
because it made me laugh.

I wish I knew about the body like he did.
My belly aches for heat.  My bones will not rest

until they are ash, until
they are moonlight and everyone can touch them.

# Aubade

*I'm less personal than, say, winter.*
        *If winter summers—*

*bangs on the drum that makes sugar sweet*
*and salt swell in mines.*

*If I could make warmth.*
*The spiritualist—the weatherman—*

                *that rings a bell with his mind*

*might storm your covered way with bramble,*
*or, like cymbals have feet, Michigan will winter.*

        *And in the spring, if at the riverbank*
                        *there's a fishery,*
*if shipbuilding and dunescapes.*

*The sun can't help.*

# Yellow Jackets

*for Amy Newman*


I've come to see the Queen's chamber,

                                the layers of honey

and paper-mâché,

             her head bowed as others serve her—

the hive is jumping.


     I wait and watch for a change in the light

or the heat or my want and one


              by one from the hive they come,


the swift curve of their stingers,

the shadow of wings,

               eyes like carnival mirrors,

as they rise off the roof

into a hard new language.

# Opera

*bedside with Mandy at Wood County Hospital*

The notch where voice originates,
where feathers like needle
points taper and abrade the flesh
until through your own speech
you find mine.  Stretch your folds,
dwell on the rolls of a whistle
where we merge,
rouse loud in the margins
so that during swallowing
confessions accent your voice
like bruises on an apple,
like blood that wells in your gums.

# Ninth Morning in a Row with Binoculars

I'm in my truck, I-94, I-80—they're all the same—
when a spring-robin flies into my cabin, knocks
off the rearview mirror and falls onto the passenger

seat, shocked, out cold, its caramel feet docile
against its chest.  I, too, am breathless, unsure
whether to pull over or throw the robin out

the window before it wakes.  How does one
resuscitate a bird?  How does one know when
to resuscitate a bird?  Two nights ago the weatherman

said, *spring is finally here*, said, *fire up those grills, folks,
it's bratwurst time!*  What an odd thing to say.
Every morning a cardinal whistles from the heavy

pine outside my bedroom, his trills enough
to stir my dogs who know the sun has risen.
I sip coffee on the porch and watch the cardinal

tease his mate, his black face, crest, how he shares
seeds by kissing her beak: perches on a fence post,
harmonizes with her, phrases with her: their banter.

Behind the house, cars race by on US-131, the whoosh
of semis, their long haul beginning or nearly ending,
and I remember baseball scores from the radio

the night before: *Chicago dismantles Houston, 9-3,
and the Pirates blow a late lead, fall 8-6 to the Marlins.*  So final.
The everyday becomes more everyday every day,

yet still I wish I could cup that robin
and breathe life back into him, but this spring
is its last, and lying on my passenger seat is the face

I fear most, face I've never touched but must
to make authentic, make other than silent.
It's asking too much to bring back the fallen:

our hands are busy enough predicting the weather,
busy enough flipping through radio stations to find
the ballgame, to find a voice that'll tell us *good pitching*

*will beat good hitting any time, and vice versa.*

# The Nightmare Where I Walk in the Forest

Sneak out to the edge toward every tree beset by frost—
        it is the nature of roots to nose into cracks—

or toward the one that looks to have dropped from me: a lung'd-tree,
        a boned-tree, globed entirely in ice.

                            The human face is hideous—
what hides there, what feeds eternally.

I exist only in the soles of my feet, in the run-off of frosted
        windows. I've met myself after death. A ghost:

in this pursuit
        I'll grow old and bury myself.

In darkness now: the place within the place where God slaps me awake
        or tendrils me down onto my back:

the wine-flood of my lids, the firewood of my eyes.

I am what wakes me, what makes me leap bareheaded.

# Forever Falling Off or Out

Maybe we've underestimated our prowess
the tiny noises we fear

Maybe our first scent was accidental
and we have yet to make habit
the hard smell of draught

Maybe a rib was not enough

Dreams are no different
than swimming for the first time,
than being wombed

Treading water is still an art
of the hands

Our stories our portraits

Maybe when the days are long
and the nights are warblers

Something about owls too

Something like flight
except for landing

Maybe when I die I'll be cast another
Maybe shade

Because after what makes us different
is what makes us tired

The fist of the first morning
its bellows

its interior
what we now call light

Maybe the aftermath of questioning
of moreover

Between dawn and dusk
is purgatorial

Maybe sing the days in the morning

Marvelous as the rib is
it'll never be the jaw

Maybe mimic waves
open mouths pretend midnight

and cover a mirror the size of the sea

# Aubade

I've noticed my fingernails grow more quickly in the wintertime,
as do fir trees, depths of feeling,

                and those winter months
that lead us here.

Why is the crow who calls from atop my roof

                     chased by blackbirds,

      harassed by robins on its way to the tree line?
What do they stand to gain by catching it?

This morning's sex was fast and cruel, like being chased.

                      I've been here before.

In every morning, there's a window looking out to the highway,

and down that highway we'll go again
to the sunlit bellies of land and land.

# DeKalb, Illinois, August 21, 2002

The corn grows audibly in the fields

---

Mice titter their way through unkempt roots as giant mechanical pickers roar to life across the county. Hot specks of dead skin and sharpened scraps of corn leaves race down my esophagus

---

From the West a train filled with potatoes heads toward the plains. In the crates, dragonfly larvae, fresh with hunger and lust, burrow into the potatoes. By the time I feel the weight of an uneaten root in my hand, the larvae will have flown away on wings of blue and green

---

In the fields, the adult dragonflies buzz over the corn in patterns mathematicians only dream of

---

After the fields have been blitzed by refrains of wind and rain, the odor of cow and horse drift through town. A drive by the fields makes it easy to understand why farm homes are usually built downwind of their plots

---

When I inhale, I taste prairie, taste the death of my tongue forthcoming

# Weather, Weather

I've been recording my greatest moments: eight hours of consecutive sleep,
four cheeseburgers in ten minutes,

                  two women in my lifetime.
It's unfortunate hurricanes only occur on the coasts
because for once I'd like to board up my windows,

                          travel inland to my in-laws,
and bunker down with licorice, a flashlight, and a weather radio.

      Perhaps it's too rash to wish for a storm, but I'm not convinced
it couldn't happen despite geography.

The Midwest, with its heart in its fists, its shortgrass prairies and placid charm,
inspires fear with its snowstorms, but I know

                    not much has changed in millions of years,
I know that my greatest moments will one day be clogged in glaciers

      and icedrifts the size of Wisconsin, and yet I still find a way to wish
for initials in wet concrete, dead leaves in my garage—

                    straight talk,
as they say, has lost its pizzazz.  So fiddle me this, why do I

                            sometimes

wish I had more to record?

# Earth's Otherwise Silence

What's holier than a Michigan winter, where only the wind seizes,
where people birthed here understand its howling,

                                        Earth's otherwise silence?


But today it's still fall—the election's over and people are outside,
not ready for sleep.


When the long night comes they'll fall to their beds,
roll a few times and settle

                        the way carved knuckle-bones do.


And the oxen will pasture through the night,
and tomorrow they'll skid logs, pull until drought takes their tongues.

# Back Home

Travelling backwards on the train from Kalamazoo to Chicago,
I solve a quadratic equation, a crossword puzzle,

my marriage—

Michigan, swollen between two lakes, is slopeless,

or cured like beef and leather:

Romanticism will always have Her cynics.

I'm young:

the trees outside the train window are bald as the man
sitting in front of me, and yet it's impossible to get this right.

# Painting Houses

This early morning's tree line,
                                    red like my son's face.
How a conductor conducts

with his hands,
and my son's crying like a flute's run:

            the high-dance of metal with skin
and before it's over, Matt-in-Tacoma

            will have wept for the first time
in twenty years,

                because finally,
synaesthesia,
                a house painted with tears.
And when will my son
                    be a maker of houses?

                When will he be old enough to ride
on my shoulders at the fair,
                        see Blue Oyster Cult
at the County Fair? *Go, Go, Godzilla!*
He won't dance. He will, however,
                            understand
that morning starts tomorrow.

*Early morning is the new late night*
and the early-night's call of bathwater
                    warming is body-splintered, bladed,
                                    still lit

and inviting: to bathe is to agree with the body's
        Heaven.  Son,
understand the groundless.  I'm here with you.


I'm head-stoned and so alive.
                                 Fatherhood has blessed
me with a transient freedom, therefore I'm
the name of a new color:
                     remorning.
      Matt-in-Tacoma's grave,
the groundwater close to boiling:
        the sun has long ago set.


My son and I will look up: have the stars
                         ever been so fevered
as when we spy them as children?

# Winter

I hardly dream of wolves
hunting, howling, barking,
and turning a dead
moose to its back, its legs cracked
at the knees, blood pooling
at the wolves' feet, steam rising
from the kill's split ribs

———————————

I hardly dream of wolves

———————————

I hardly ever dream,
hardly ever of the womb

———————————

I am not that far removed
from cracking bones
to put food in my stomach,
from dipping my nose
into the gut of a moose
to warm my face from the cold

———————————

I am not that far removed
from eating only what I catch

———————————

I am not that far removed
from being afraid of waking
to find my family vanished

# Too Damn Perfect

I'm trying to translate my misgivings into precipitation
that isn't snow,
                 but the night's so dark my hands won't work
and my breath turns to frost in front of the open window.

April and November are sometimes interchangeable
like PVC piping and fallopian tubes,
or sons and daughters:
                         both a deck of cards and a river
can be shuffled. Both love and quiet can be forgiven.

# Acknowledgments

Grateful acknowledgement is made to the following journals where the following poems first appeared, though some in different forms:

*Barn Owl Review*: "Aubade (Sunlight through clouds…)" and "Aubade (And it's morning…)"
*Bat City Review*: "All Stones Are Broken Stones"
*Boxcar Poetry Review*: "A Miscarriage Scare at Bronson Methodist"
*Colorado Review*: "Forever Falling Off or Out"
*Controlled Burn*: "If you've never seen the devil"
*DIAGRAM*: "A Poem about My Father Will Always Begin *My Father*" (as "Shuttlecock")
*diode*: "Tornado Warning" and "Divorce"
*DMQ Review*: "My Ill-lit Something" and "And She's Fallen"
*The Eleventh Muse*: "DeKalb, Illinois, August 21, 2002"
*Front Porch*: "Aubade (I've been thinking…)" and "Aubade (I'm less personal…)"
*Grist: The Journal for Writers*: "Love" (as "A Love Poem")
*The Laurel Review*: "The Nightmare Where I Walk in the Forest"
*Lumina*: "Back Home"
*Memorious*: "Winter" and "Nectar"
*New England Review*: "Aubade (Look for me…)" and "Ninth Morning in a Row with Binoculars"
*Night Train*: "Aubade (I've noticed…)"
*Ninth Letter*: "Ovaries" and "Opera" (as "If You Love Opera")
*No Tell Motel*: "Yellow Jackets" and "Snorkeling"
*Parthenon West Review*: "Blackbirds"
*The Pinch*: "Notes from a Sleepwalker"
*Quarterly West*: "How to Say *I Love You*" and "Aubade (Forty-four hours…)"
*Redactions*: "Lake Big Arbor Vitae"
*Reed*: "Father, there are poets"
*RHINO*: "Orgasm"
*Salt Hill*: "A Feeding"
*The Yalobusha Review*: "Tricycle"

"Ninth Morning in a Row with Binoculars" was featured at *Poetry Daily*, October 2, 2008.

"How to Say *I Love You*" was featured at *Verse Daily*, March 25, 2010.

Some of these poems appear in the chapbook, *They Speak of Fruit* (Cooper Dillon Books, 2009).

# Special Acknowledgments

Thank you to my friends and family. Thank you to Northern Illinois University, Bowling Green State University, and Western Michigan University. Thank you to the poets, classmates, and peers who have read and reread these poems in manuscript form: Michael Cherry, Adam Clay, Nancy Eimers, Andrea England, Nate Haldeman, Keith Montesano, William Olsen, Julie Platt, F. Daniel Rzicznek, Chad Sweeney, Jennifer K. Sweeney, Larissa Szporluk, and the list goes on.

Thank you to J.P. Dancing Bear for choosing and believing in this book. Thank you to Frank Cuccairre for this beautiful cover, his ecstatic vision.

A very loving thanks to my wife, Mandy, to our son, Auden, and to the little peapod we'll meet soon enough. And thank you, Dad. Thank you, Mom Weland.

Thank you Alex Lemon and David Baker.

And finally a very special thank you to Amy Newman. This book would not exist with you, A-bird. Thank you for your guidance, your support, and your friendship.

# About the Author

**Gary L. McDowell** is the author of two chapbooks, *They Speak of Fruit* (Cooper Dillon, 2009) and *The Blueprint* (Pudding House, 2005) and co-editor, with F. Daniel Rzicznek, of *The Rose Metal Press Field Guide to Prose Poetry: Contemporary Poets in Discussion and Practice* (Rose Metal Press, 2010). His poems have appeared in journals such as *Bellingham Review, Colorado Review, Indiana Review, Laurel Review, New England Review, Ninth Letter, Quarterly West,* and elsewhere. He currently lives in Kalamazoo, MI with his wife, Mandy, and their young son, Auden, where he's finishing his PhD in American Literature and Contemporary Poetry at Western Michigan University.

www.ingramcontent.com/pod-product-compliance
Lightning Source LLC
Chambersburg PA
CBHW022030090426
42739CB00006BA/369